GROWING A HEALTHY VEGETABLE GARDEN FOR BEGINNERS

THE FASTEST AND SIMPLE STEP BY STEP DIRECTION FOR GROWING A FRUIT OR VEGETABLE FROM SEED TO EAT

LISA TIMOTHY

COPYRIGHT

INTRODUCTION

There is this joy that comes when we connect with nature. In the morning when we jog we feel nature's serenity refreshing us through the day. Growing a vegetable garden is a great way to nourish our bodies with the best sources of food. In a rating of 5, you'll be 4 times free of chemicals if you consume produce from a garden. Having a vegetable garden gives you easy access to decide what to plant, prepare the seedlings, plant, monitor the crops, harvest and feast on the harvested produce. You know the kind of unending joy that comes with entering your garden to pluck fresh tomatoes or picking up carrots for an evening refreshment – it feels so good.

It's important to decide the purpose of having a vegetable garden. Having a purpose is the motivation that keeps you well going in starting and maintaining the garden. If you would like to have your vegetable garden for personal consumption, then it's all good. If your garden is for family consumption, then its fine as you can have more hands to help you in the garden. You may as well decide to plant for commercial purposes and sell off the produce. It's a good way to have an alternative source of income. Do you know that by planting seeds in polythene bags and pots, you can raise thousands of seedlings and sell them at market standard prices? Yes, it's very doable. You only need to know the right dots to connect. Focus as we explore together, how to join the lines for starting a vegetable garden.

CHAPTER ONE

Basic Things You Need to Know to Start Your First Vegetable Garden

Vegetable gardening is a lot simpler than you might think, it requires time, resources, and some research. Growing a vegetable garden is a good way to get in touch with your green side. The process of keeping your vegetable garden is rewarding as you can grow a lot of healthy foods for you, your family, neighbours, or for sale. What you need to grow the perfect vegetable garden is time and patience. There could be no greater method to act naturally adequate than by developing your own food. Its fun, fulfilling, and the vegetables taste such a great deal better compared to the store. You may feel that growing a vegetable seems like a lot of work, or that you can keep nothing alive so for what reason would you even attempt, plant vegetables during the right seasons so you don't have to fear cultivating.

Picking which vegetables to grow: There are countless vegetables to browse so the thing I suggest is going with a rundown of your top picks and afterward checking whether that vegetable grows well in your general vicinity. There are heaps of things you need to consider with regards to vegetable cultivating. Among these are the readiness of soil, vegetable cultivating strategies, an ideal opportunity to plant, and what vegetables to plant. You ought to be cautious about when to plant vegetables as you can't simply plant any time you need. This is the reason it is significant that you concentrate first and do some exploration about cultivating before you continue on firing up your own vegetable ranch.

You can likewise plant a wide range of vegetables and collect them to sell or make into various items. No vegetable garden can be fruitful except if the land is overseen and adequately cared for. In case you're totally new to planting or potentially beginning another garden without any preparation, this is a great time for you to begin.

To start a vegetable garden, there are certain things you need to pay attention to. They include:

Start with a small garden: You need to know that starting small helps you master the dos and don'ts better as a first-timer. Agriculture requires an understanding of scientific and natural processes. When you start with a small garden, you'll easily learn the processes that are involved in planting, harvesting, and storing the produce. The ideas and lessons you learn from the small garden will equate to guide and nurture to manage a big garden. If you start with a small garden, this allows starting planting in your backyard or having pots placed on spaces in the backyard of the house.

Grow what you love: The freedom that comes with starting your vegetable garden is your regular flex on decision making. When you own your garden, the decision-making power lies with you. You can decide to plant tomatoes, carrots, spinach, or even green beans. The choice is yours to make when it comes to what you can plant. This is where your needs or that of your family comes in. If as a family, you enjoy carrots in your food, then you can have a chemical-free carrot planted, and harvested just in your backyard.

Choose a spot for your garden: To have the best of experience in small-scale farming at home, it's essential to have a good location for your crops. Choose a space around your compound especially your backyard that is cool and where shade can be for the crops. When planted crops have shade, they perform better and bear fruits. You should choose a location that is close to the water supply, accessible, and at least 10 feet away from the wall of the house. Choosing an accessible place to plant makes it possible for you to move in tools, fertilizers, or pesticides as and when needed. You should choose a place where sunlight can easily reach the vegetables. Sunlight and temperature are required for good vegetable growth.

Testing and fixing your soil: If you want a result-oriented planting on your vegetable garden, then it's best to test your soil for its composition and fix the soil where it's needed. Testing the soil makes you know the quantity and quality in terms of nutrient, alkalinity, and acidity. You can hire a soil expert to draw soil samples from your backyard and run laboratory tests on the soil. You can apply homemade techniques including testing for sand, silt, and clay using an empty jar for soil testing, do a pantry pH test to measure alkalinity or acidity in the soil, and taking soil samples to see the number of earthworms in the soil. Having up to 10 earthworms in the sample is an indication of a well-fertilized soil. The results of the test help you select the right variety of crops that matches the soil type.

Provide plenty of water: You need to know that just as humans need water to live, vegetables need a consistent water supply to live as well. Good soil is the premise of healthy plants. Watering vegetables appropriately is fundamental to keep a healthy and bountiful garden. Knowing how and when to water your vegetable garden will guarantee that those little crops you've grown will grow up to become energetic and produce lovely blossoms and tasty foods. Water your seedlings with room temperature water. Your soil should not be excessively hot or excessively cold. Ensure you monitor your vegetable garden and soil moisture frequently. Watering your vegetable garden at the right time would give you abundant produce. Watering your veggie garden could be a tremendous torment during the heat of summer, there's no uncertainty about the best time to water your crops you should use water sprinklers but ensure to always check on soil moisture to figure out the best time to water your crops. The ideal time to water plants could be when it is dry but it should not be done in all cases. To water vegetables effectively, you need to figure out water system necessity under climate conditions. Water for a long time, and create an atmosphere for micro-organisms. Water pretty much nothing and roots become shallow. Water in the evening and bugs come out to eat. Water from excessively high and a large portion of the dampness is lost to evaporation. In case you're watering by hand, make certain to point the progression of water at the base of plants where it's required. Ensure to point your watering can carefully hit the ground, not the plant. Try not to water on windy days as you might miss your watering direction.

Ensure you water your plants at the Right Time. You have to ensure that adequate water is supplied to the garden to yield a maximal crop returns.

Know what to plant: Most plants need space and if you don't allow them to have their own little piece of an area, there might be a long-haul of challenges growing a healthy vegetable garden. Be practical with your goal to starting your garden, start by measuring your garden space. Measure up your garden space and apportion the type of vegetation you intend to do, it could be a mixed vegetable garden or a specific vegetable garden, but whichever one you prefer it should be sorted from the beginning. Set nursery boundaries and beds for your crops to enable you to achieve your planting plan. Ensure you know your soil's pH levels (Acidic or Alkaline), to know the best crop that can grow in your area or season. You can purchase basic pH test soil packs to give insightful data to base your planting plan around. Utilize good seeds for your vegetable garden and ensure that you have a planting calendar put in place to help you always grow the right crops based on your soil typography or climate condition. Some valuable planting schedules can assist you with deciding your environmental zone and appropriate planting guide. Some veggies will not do well in the summer heat, while others flourish in a chilly climate. It's a misuse of assets to plant at some unacceptable time. Planting both cool and warm-climate vegetables will give you a collection of vegetables and spices persistently through the spring, summer, and fall. Tomatoes, spinach, kale, radish, zucchini, green beans, lettuce, collards, carrots, mustard greens, Peppers are easy veggies, to begin within your vegetable garden. Nutrient-rich and soil-friendly vegetables that you can plant include lettuce, green beans, radishes, tomatoes, zucchini, peppers, carrots, chard, spinach, kale, and peas.

CHAPTER TWO

Reasons for Growing Vegetables, Herbs and Fruits

Growing vegetables, herbs, and fruits in your garden helps you in many ways. Apart from the flexibility of choice of crops to plant, you benefit from the freshness and nice flavour from produce harvested in the garden. This means that when you plant in your garden, you have created access to fresh tomatoes, carrots, and radishes directly from the garden. The flavour is there 100% with no mixture or saturation. It's just as best as you can have it – fresh from the soil.

Instead of having to buy peppers, spinach, kale, and peas from the market, having a vegetable garden brings you financial comfort to save your money. Vegetables needed by your family can be harvested right from your backyard into your kitchen. This makes you save money for vegetables for another home or personal need. Numerous benefits come with growing your vegetable garden some of which are mentioned below.

Fit and green: You have the opportunity to keep fit when you work in your garden. Your vegetable garden in your compound doesn't only make you save cost or have fresh produce, it also makes you work out as you prepare the soil, plant, water, weed, monitor, and harvest in your garden. By applying fertilizer or pesticide, you take minutes running into hours of work to ensure that the planted crops are well managed. By so doing, you burn calories. This helps you maintain your weight and avoid obesity. You can decide to only work on your farm on cool evenings. The fact that it's right in your backyard or close to your window motivates you to work on the garden and have yourself in good health.

Healthier option: When you plant your vegetables, herbs, and fruits in your garden, you immediately come off the worries of "is this safe to eat?" or that of "is this chemical not too much." The benefit of owning a vegetable garden is that you eat produce that is chemical-free, organic, and naturally taken from the garden. When you see news or read about the spiralling danger of chemicals in the food we eat, you realize that there's an increase in the carcinogenic level resulting from vegetable consumption. This indicates that the planting, growing, storing and processing of vegetables now revolves around chemicals that are grossly inimical to health. Having your vegetables from your garden makes you stay off worries of chemicals and radiant in the freshness of 'directly from the soil vegetables.'

Waste reduction: You reduce food waste if you own a vegetable garden. This means that you can freely pluck the needed quantity of tomatoes or peppers for a particular meal. If you're making lunch or dinner, having a garden makes you move to the garden without restriction, harvest the needed quantity of carrots and spinach that the food requires. By this, you cut down on food wastage. If you had bought a pack of carrots from a supermarket and didn't finish it, the available is prone to wastage – a garden makes you free from the shackle of food wastage.

More Nutrients: When you eat the right quantity of vegetables, herbs, and fruits, you make a good nutrient choice for your health and that of your family. Eating a good combination of fruits, vegetables and herbs makes you and your family free from a heart attack, stroke, and cancer. The combination is rich in fiber and potassium which are essential for the healthy development of an individual.

Consistent food supply: The plan to start your vegetable garden leaves you with numerous benefits, one of which is continuous food supplies. You would never run out of nutritious food consistently. You can also earn consistent cash flow from your vegetable garden. You can eat, store for the future, with the option to sell your excess at market stands or transform it into jam, oils, cleansers, or a wide scope of other regular items. Food banks, neighbours, your community, and asylums seekers are regularly needing new produce your vegetable garden could go a long way to help those in need. You can accommodate your local area with the most healthy and nutritious food supplies.

CHAPTER THREE

A Guide to Start Your Vegetable Garden

Now that you have identified the reasons for having a vegetable garden. You should do that now if you haven't done it before now. You also need to keep in mind the basics for starting a garden mentioned in the opening chapter. By now you need no reminder that you will need to choose a suitable location for the vegetables to thrive. You need to ensure that the following is well achieved to have a productive garden.

Making your vegetable garden: in making your garden, you need to do clearing if there is a bush in your backyard. You should also level the ground in the backyard to suit the purpose of the planting you want to make. If you're planting tomatoes, you may have to first clear, level the soil, and make a nursery bird for the seeds. When the seeds begin to germinate, then you can transplant them into the main soil. After this, you ensure to regulate watering and monitoring. You can then be sure of healthy produce from this exercise.

Improving soil before you plant: when you test your soil, you will get results that indicate whether the soil is loamy, sandy, or clayey. The tests will also show the acidity and alkalinity level of the soil. Importantly, the nutrient level of the soil is measured. From the results, you have to decide the level of improvement to have on the soil for a good crop practice. To improve the soil, for a clayey soil, you should add compost, peat moss, and coarse sand; for a sandy soil, you should add nitrogen, sawdust peat moss, manure and humus. You can treat soil alkalinity with ground sulfur application while you take care of soil acidity with the application of ground stone that's well-grounded. You can add organic matter to improve the nutrient in the soil.

Getting ready to plant: when you have decided on what to plant. You may plant tomatoes, carrots, or even peppers. After this decision, you prepare the soil. If the soil requires preliminary watering, then you can water it to prepare for planting. Make sure the variety of vegetables you're planting is compatible with the soil.

Caring for your vegetable garden: when you look at the extent of efforts you're putting into starting your own garden, you'll realize that you've to consistently monitor and care for the garden. To prevent plant death, you have to carefully water the crops and weed. You need to remove plants that may cause growth delay for your planted vegetable. If the garden needs expert assistance for soil or crops, then you can hire the service of an expert for that. Caring for your garden is a way to make sure you benefit from your efforts, time, and resources put into starting a vegetable garden.

CHAPTER FOUR

Low Maintenance Vegetables, Garden Fruits and Plants

Remember that maintenance of your garden is quintessential to its sustenance and productivity. If you don't remove weed your garden, then you may be leaving your planted potatoes at the mercy of weeds that may eventually exterminate what you have planted.

To get the best results from your garden, you have to:

Quantity-Quality: starting with a minimal quantity of plants will help you to easily monitor the process and harvest without difficulties. If you stay alone or with an aged person who isn't required to undergo stress at most times, you may consider filling pots with soil and spreading tomato seedlings. You can have ten selected pots, then soil-fill it and begin to plant your tomatoes. This doesn't require tilling the ground or labouring to clear the bush. It is seamless to practice as you can use your leisure time to pick weeds from the pots. Minimal quantity is close to maximal quality.

Grow only what you will eat: it is apt to be conscious of the fact that as you want an alternative to fresh food, you also want to maintain the aesthetics of your home. With this, the best way to maintain home beauty is to plant a bulk that can sustain your family. A large quantity of vegetables, herbs, and fruits can make the house watery if not well organized. To avoid losing your fashion taste to food taste, you should plant a quantity that can cater to your home at a time.

Build a raised bed or square foot garden: if you want to plant potatoes or tomatoes, then you'll need to prepare the soil and make a bed. For a good tomato planting, you may have to prepare a nursery bed in your backyard. If there is not so much space, you then may have to use trays to spread the tomato seedlings. You can also have the tomato seedlings in a plastic bag or pot and transplant them after 6-8 weeks. It's important to know that you should gradually expose the planted seedlings in the nursery to sunlight before transplanting to prepare them for the actual experience on the soil outdoor. You can make a square foot garden for outdoor planting.

Choose easy vegetables: your choice of vegetables influences your workload, tools, and the water supply level to the garden. Some easy vegetables you can plant as a beginner include radish, potatoes, spring onions, runner beans, beetroot, garlic, and tomatoes. Artichoke, celery, and muskmelon are however not as easy to plant as other vegetables are. The fact that they need steady moisture, water, and the temperature keeps the gardener on his toes to maintain the vegetables,

Weed and water: regular weeding saves the vegetables from dying. A regular water supply helps the survival and good growth of the plants. Devise means to have a consistent water supply in your garden. This is where the choice you make in selecting a location for your garden comes to reality.

CHAPTER FIVE

Building Your Vegetable Garden

The location of your garden determines how you design it. If your garden is right in your backyard, and your house is well fenced, then you have a restricted level of pest attack to the garden. If your apartment is minimally fenced and can be easily accessed by higher pests or anyone, then you can use wood and iron net to carve a boundary for your garden. This makes you be in charge while preventing intrusion into your garden. You have to ensure that you make the garden be at a place with shade. Vegetable growth requires a cool environment with good moisture. Make water tanks available in your vegetable garden. Create a space where you can work on the garden. Make pathways for in and out accessibility to the garden. It's superb to have an interesting partner to work with in the garden. With a happy partner, you don't feel the gardening stress.

When considering the construction of your garden you need to make ensure that your garden is well constructed because this is the first step towards food security. I have heard tales of farmers who planted vegetables in their backyard and their produce was damaged by animals who love vegetables, it may seem funny but imagine the hard work put into setting up your vegetable garden and there is no fruit to show for all your labour. Now let's solve the issue with this little information.

Garden Proof Enclosure: You can create your own vegetable bed or you can purchase instant things going from basic bloom beds to wooden blossom beds with capacity under them and surprisingly high self-cleaning frameworks. Vegetable nurseries need a great deal of light, place the bed in a zone that gets sun for the greater part of the day. To improve the drainage system and keep weeds from growing up into the nursery, eliminate the grass underneath the bed and do the groundwork before adding soil. The initial step to making the enclosure for your garden is by estimating the whole region you need to encase, at that point permit a 6-foot-4 to have the option to stand up in the nursery. This would bring about a 12 ft. wide by 24 ft. long and 8 ft. high construction. The objective is to be consistently comfortable when in the garden. Assemble each side of the fence exclusively. To begin with, at that point put the center posts in. Utilize 2×4 boards and spot them on a level plane along with the posts, one somewhat over mostly up and the other on the top. Make sure each side is upright. Place three of the boards along the highest point of the construction to make a rooftop, going from scene post and secure them with screws. Ensure that the enclosure is safe enough to keep squirrels and other animals out, while it is easier for you to get in. Along these lines, utilizing a similar scene post for a casing, construct an entryway. Cut two of the 12 ft. boards into four equivalent pieces and two longer side pieces utilizing a miter saw. Create a square shape outline with a cross help in the center, associating the pieces with pocket openings. When the edge and the entryway have been assembled, put a layer of grade wood finish to blend with the environment. Use bird netting or something stronger like steel hardware to wrap your garden enclosure.

CHAPTER SIX

Planting Your Vegetables

After you have made a choice of how to set up your garden, and have decided on what to plant. You prepare the soil and make a nursery bed where needed. Then you can begin to transfer seeds to the soil for permanent planting. It's the preparation of the soil and seeds that matters at the pre-planting stage. At the planting stage, it's the planted seeds that matter and has to be watered and weeded. Then you keep up with the crops monitoring. At the post-planting stage, you focus on how to efficiently store the vegetables harvested from your garden.

Plant in the right area: Pick an area for your vegetable garden by observing these: a place that has good soil moisture, has a lot of sun as vegetables need about 7 hours of sunlight daily, abundant space, and closeness to your hose or water source.

Select your choice of veggies: Choose the right vegetables if you want to enjoy abundant produce based on the following criteria: plant-based for your environment, space, tastes, and level of skill. Rookies might need to think about a portion of the simpler harvests to develop, similar to carrots, beans, cucumbers, peppers, and lettuce.

Set up the needed soil moisture: Blend manure and regular composts into your garden space to condition the soil to get ready to accommodate and nourish all your crops. You can consult an expert on the right soil composition that would help give you the best yield

Develop a planting guide: Planting cycles are diverse based on plant and seasons, so you ought not to plant every one of the seeds simultaneously. Planting dates can be found on seed bundles. Survey the ideal conditions for every veggie you need to plant before making a planting plan.

Keep the weeds out: The beauty of a garden can be hidden by weeds, these unwanted guests could cover the awesome landscape of your vegetable garden. Mulching is the best method to control weeds. Add a 2-to 4-inch-thick layer of natural mulch to your garden to hold the weeds back from overwhelming your yields. There are times weeds prove difficult to remove, this is when you uproot them from their roots manually, snatch them low on their stems and yank forcefully, making a point to extricate the whole root.

CHAPTER SEVEN

Maintaining and Harvesting Your Vegetables

Maintenance of your garden is paramount to making a good planting returns from your garden. You have to ensure that the water supply to the garden isn't obstructed. Vegetables need water to maintain the moisture needed for good growth. Make sure you mulch the garden to boost soil health and ensure functional soil performance and healthy vegetables. You must constantly prune out weed from the garden. If you allow weeds to grow alongside your vegetables, then you deny your lettuce, the needed soil nutrients. Instead of the lettuce having the nutrients to itself for growth, the nutrient is shared between the lettuce and the weed. You should avoid that. When your plants such as radish, onions, and carrots begin to spread their wings in your garden, it's best to carefully shed the spreading to maintain the growth of other vegetables in the garden. You can apply fertilizer to improve the nitrogen, potassium, and phosphorus of the soil to boost the growth and freshness of the vegetables. When it comes to harvesting, you need to ensure that you pick your vegetables as fresh from the garden. Picking fresh carrots, peppers, and tomatoes from the garden makes you achieve your set purpose to eat fresh, chemical-free farm produce. Fresh vegetables also give to nice flavour and natural taste that you can never imagine. With the naturalness, you move into the realms of healthy growth, refreshed skin, and effective functionality of all organs of the body. Vegetables make you easily get protein, carbohydrates, sodium, potassium, and other nutrients needed for good growth.

Daily garden check: At the point when your garden starts to grow, it is required you do a plant audit consistently, by this, I mean check soil moisture, climate conditions, sun exposure, water levels, crop appearance, weed, pest control, and others to ensure your vegetable garden is positioned to yield bountifully. It is essential to check your garden daily to enable you to fix any issue that might affect your vegetable garden before they happen.

Pick smaller vegetables: Make sure you do not wait for when your produce grows so big before you consider them for harvest. Have you at any point gone to pick a carrot and it appears to be the size of a watermelon? That is not in reality great. Try not to stand by until your vegetables become too enormous. It is ideal to pick produce when it's little. This is the time most vegetables are at their delicate stages and have better flavour, and haven't created numerous seeds. Notwithstanding, if you do stumble into a big vegetable pick them and use them and process them into other food varieties. The ideal vegetable is ready for harvest at about 6-8 inches long. Harvest your produce in batches to make the process easier and enjoyable.

Harvest with care: You have waited too long for your crops to yield, this is not the time to harvest carelessly, you need to also take caution at this point. Reaping is an incredible task that you do not want to allocate to anyone around you or someone that is not knowledgeable. Ensure those helping you know that harvest time is delicate. If you need your family or friend's assistance, make a point to remind them to be delicate with the produce. Vegetables can be easily crushed. It is imperative to delicately pick them and spot them in a container or can.

Watch your Step: Weeds could sometimes cover the pathway to your garden. It is significant you watch where you step when you are collecting your vegetables. Your garden can be tight to move in. Accordingly, you'll need to ensure you either have clear walkways, or you watch where you put your feet.

CONCLUSION

It's not enough to complain about the sandy form of the vegetables you just bought from the supermarket. Instead of complaining, then you should control what you buy, and eat by owning a vegetable garden. To own a vegetable garden, however, you need to know how-to, the dos, and the don'ts. Mastering the breakdown of how to start your own vegetable garden makes you a master of your ship when it comes to healthy eating. You need to make a choice of location and decide what to plant. You have to test the soil and ensure it's compatible with your vegetable choice. If not, you can naturally treat the soil or hire a soil expert to treat the soil for you. If you're planting tomatoes, you may have to first make a nursery bed before transplanting. You need to regularly water the plants, weed, and harvest as and when due- when the vegetables are fresh, spicy, and of inviting flavour.

Vegetables you can plant round the year are kale, radicchio, onions, horseradish, artichoke, chayote squash, okra, eggplant, peppers, and tomatoes.